The Library of the Five Senses & the Sixth Sense™

Touch

Sue Hurwitz

The Rosen Publishing Group's
PowerKids Press™
New York

Published in 1997 by The Rosen Publishing Group, Inc.
29 East 21st Street, New York, NY 10010

First Edition

Book Design: Kim Sonsky

Photo Credits: Cover and all photo illustrations by Seth Dinnerman.

Hurwitz, Sue, 1934–
   Touch / by Sue Hurwitz.
      p.   cm. — (Library of the five senses & the sixth sense)
   Includes index.
   Summary: Explains the sense of touch, including a discussion of the skin and nerve endings.
   ISBN 0-8239-5054-9
   1. Touch—Juvenile literature. [1. Touch. 2. Senses and sensation. 3. Skin.] I. Title. II. Series: Hurwitz, Sue, 1934– Library of the five senses (& the sixth sense)
QP451.H87 1997
612.8'8—dc21
                                  96–29960
                                       CIP
                                        AC

Manufactured in the United States of America

CONTENTS

Robbie

Robbie likes to play at the beach. He feels dry, gritty sand under his bare feet. He feels the warm sunshine on his body. He touches the hard shells in the sand. Robbie feels his skin get hot.

He walks into the ocean and splashes cool water over his body. Then he feels something squishy between his toes. What could it be? He reaches into the water and pulls out a big piece of seaweed!

5

What Is Touch?

Touch is one of your **senses** (SEN-sez). Your senses tell you what is happening to you. They also tell you about the world around you. Your sense of touch tells you how things feel.

You get touch messages from all over your body. But your sense of touch is greater in some parts of your body than others. You feel more with your fingertips and your lips than your knees and elbows. Your sense of touch is strongest at the tip of your tongue.

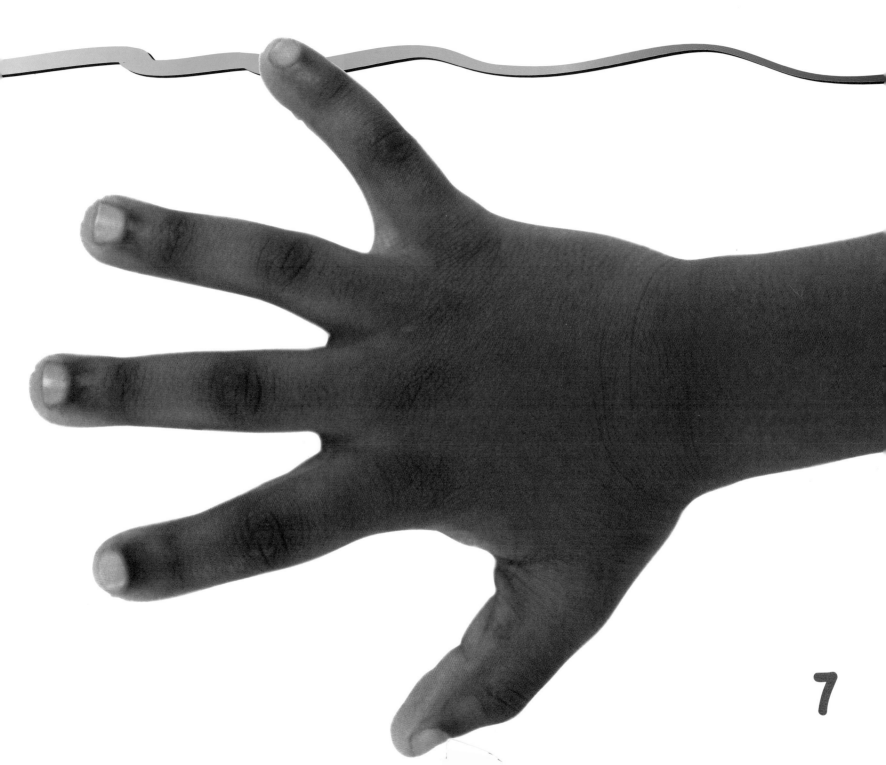

7

How Do You Touch?

You touch with your skin. Your skin has millions of **nerve endings** (NERV EN-dings). These nerve endings are tiny touch **receptors** (re-SEP-terz). Touch receptors are right underneath or inside your skin.

Touch receptors send messages about the things you touch to

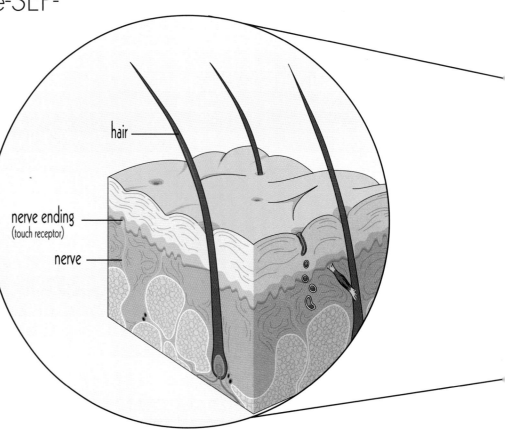

hair

nerve ending
(touch receptor)

nerve

8

your **brain** (BRAYN). They tell you if something is hard or soft. They tell you if something is hot or cold. They tell you if something feels heavy or light.

Your Skin

Did you know that skin is the biggest **organ** (OR-gun) of your body? Skin is also **elastic** (ee-LAS-tik). That means it lets you move your body in different ways. Skin covers your whole body. It also covers the inside of your mouth and nose. Skin protects you. It helps to keep **microbes** (MY-krohbz), or germs, from getting inside your body and making you sick.

Skin does not have the same thickness all over your body. It is thicker on the bottoms of your feet and on the palms of your hands. Your skin is thinnest on your eyelids.

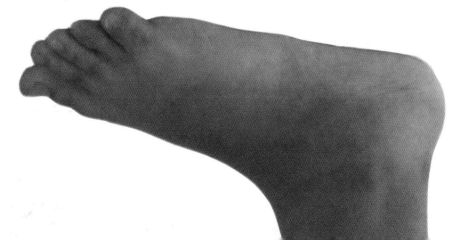

11

Parts of Your Skin

Your skin has two **layers** (LAY-erz). The top layer is called the **epidermis** (EP-ih-DER-mis). It has tiny tough, dead cells. They flake or rub off all the time. But this doesn't hurt you. Your skin is so thick that you don't even feel it.

The layer of skin below the epidermis is called the **dermis** (DER-mis). Your touch receptors are in the dermis. The dermis has hair roots and **oil glands** (OYL GLANDZ). It also has **blood vessels** (BLUD VES-ulz) and **sweat glands** (SWET GLANDZ). Below the epidermis and dermis is a layer of fat.

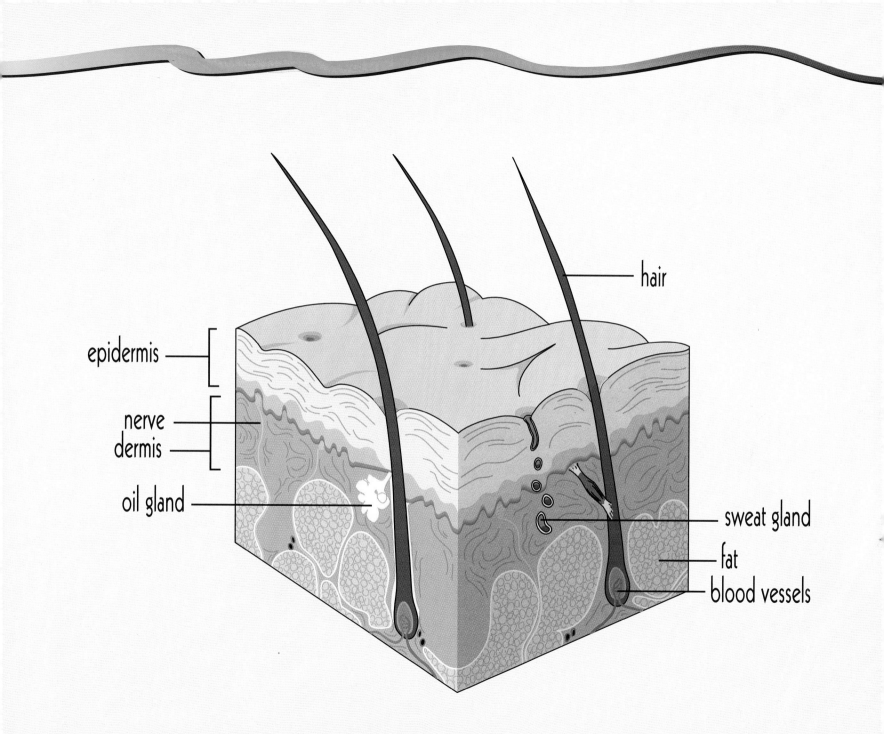

epidermis

nerve

dermis

oil gland

hair

sweat gland

fat

blood vessels

Nails and Hair

The fingernails and toenails on your body are made of special cells in your epidermis. This tough, waterproof material is called **keratin** (KER-uh-tin). Nails are made of a very thick layer of keratin. Nails protect the ends of your fingers and toes.

Hair roots are made of keratin too. You have thousands of hairs on your head and all over your body. The hair on your head is thick and protects it from the sun. Your eyebrows and eyelashes protect your eyes.

Touch and Your Brain

When you touch things, your receptors send messages to your brain. Your brain **interprets** (in-TER-prets) the information that your nerve endings send it. That information is turned into thoughts that you can understand. This all happens very, very quickly.

Then your brain tells you what to do. If you've touched something that feels nice, such as a rabbit's fur or cool water on a hot day, your brain tells you that you like the way it feels and it's okay to keep touching that thing. If you have touched something harmful, such as a hot stove, your brain tells you to move away from it.

17

Touch and Pain

Your sense of touch tells you about pain that might come from what's happening around you. Pain warns you that something is wrong. Receptors that tell you about pain are in the top part of the dermis. This can help keep you from getting hurt or burned.

There are many kinds of pain. Pain may be dull or aching or pain may be sharp or throbbing. People can help you better when you tell them where and how you are hurting.

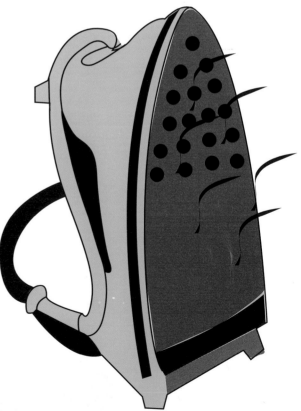

Skin and Your Health

Your body grows new skin cells all the time. Eating healthy foods helps you grow healthy new cells. Your old skin cells move up to the top of your epidermis. Then new cells from the dermis move up to take their place.

When you cut yourself, **platelets** (PLAYT-lets) in your blood form a scab to protect your cut or sore. Then as new skin cells grow over the cut or sore, the scab falls off. Make sure you don't pick or pull at a scab before it falls off on its own. This could form a scar, and the scarred area of skin is less sensitive to touch than before.

Sometimes a bandage will help a cut or sore heal.

21

Skin Care

The best way to make sure that you will be able to touch and feel things the way you're supposed to is by taking good care of your skin.

- A cut on your skin could allow germs into your body. Wash cuts or sores as soon as possible.
- It's important to keep your body clean. Dirty skin allows germs to grow. Always wash your hands before you eat or handle food.
- Too much sun may overheat your body or burn your skin. Try not to spend too much time in the sun and drink plenty of water.
- Be sure to wear sunscreen if you are going to be in the sun. Skin can burn easily.

Take care of your skin and it will help you feel lots of things!

Glossary

blood vessel (BLUD VES-ul) A tiny tunnel in your body through which blood flows.

brain (BRAYN) The main nerve center in your head. The brain controls everything that your body does.

dermis (DER-mis) The layer of skin under the epidermis. Touch receptors are in the dermis.

elastic (ee-LAS-tik) Something able to stretch and spring back to its original shape.

epidermis (EP-ih-DER-mis) The outer layer of skin that often flakes and rubs off.

interpret (in-TER-pret) To change from one kind of information to another to better understand something.

keratin (KER-uh-tin) The hard material that makes up your fingernails and toenails.

layer (LAY-er) A thickness of some material.

microbe (MY-krohb) A germ.

nerve ending (NERV EN-ding) The end of a rope-like cell that acts as a receptor in your skin.

oil gland (OYL GLAND) A tiny sack that makes and releases oil.

organ (OR-gun) One part of the body that has its own special functions.

platelets (PLAYT-lets) Part of the blood that helps to form a scab.

receptor (re-SEP-ter) Tiny nerve ending in or just under your skin.

senses (SEN-sez) The ways your body learns what is happening to you and the world around you.

sweat gland (SWET GLAND) A tiny sack that makes and releases sweat.

23

Index